WORKING
Children

Working Children

Carol Saller

 Carolrhoda Books, Inc./Minneapolis

To George and Arthea Saller, with love and thanks

Front cover: Sitting on wooden crates, an eight-year-old girl puts caps on cans in a Mississippi factory.
Back cover: In 1908 in Indianapolis, Indiana, a boy shines shoes.
Page one: Young workers stand outside a glass factory in Washington, D.C.
Page two: A cotton mill "spinner" poses for the camera in Macon, Georgia, in 1910.
Opposite page: Boys work at a cannery.

Text copyright © 1998 by Carol Saller

Carolrhoda Books, Inc., c/o The Lerner Publishing Group
241 First Avenue North, Minneapolis, MN 55401 U.S.A.

Website address: www.lernerbooks.com

LIBRARY OF CONGRESS CATALOGING-IN-PUBLICATION

Saller, Carol.
    Working children / Carol Saller.
        p.   cm. — (Picture the American past)
    Includes bibliographical references (p.) and index.
    Summary: Describes the various jobs which children performed during the early
1900s, the reasons for employment, working conditions, the efforts of reformers, and
child labor today.
    ISBN 1-57505-276-8
    1. Children—Employment—United States—History—Juvenile literature.
[1. Children—Employment.] I. Title. II. Series.
HD6250.U3S2   1998
331.3'4'0973—dc21   97-51272

Manufactured in the United States of America
1 2 3 4 5 6 – JR – 03 02 01 00 99 98

CONTENTS

Above: Miss Helen and Miss Dorothy Gould carry balloons on a walk with their mother and a friend.
Opposite page: Two girls take a break from sewing clothes in Somerville, Massachusetts, in August 1912.

A Time When Children Worked

. . . And the man had need of the children;
He gathered them in like sheep
And set them to work to earn his bread,
For children are many—and cheap.
            —from "A Song of the Factory,"
                by James F. Montague, 1913

In the early 1900s, children went to school and played with friends. They spent long summers in the sun, swimming and fishing and playing ball. They ate ice cream and read books and caught bugs. Their houses were kept warm with coal fires in the winter. They had good food to eat and nice clothes to wear.

But at the same time, there were many poor children who had and did none of these things. They didn't know how to read. They didn't have time to play. Some of them rarely saw the summer sun.

A young girl picks potatoes.

These children had to work all day, six days a week, all the year round. They worked in the factories, in the coal mines, and in the fields, sometimes for 12 hours without stopping. In the year 1900, over two million American children under the age of 16 had jobs.

McDonald, West Virginia. A young coal miner stands outside the mine in 1908.

Why did so many children work? Most of them came from poor families who needed the money.

Often children were happy to start working. They thought it would be fun to miss school. They thought they would be grown up and have money.

But they soon learned that working was not fun. They made very little money. People hired children because they could pay young workers much less than they paid adults. It was easy to frighten a child into working hard. For many children, work became a kind of prison.

River Fall, Massachusetts. A view of the spinning room at the Cornell Mill

Mines and Mills, Factories and Fields

I am so tired that I only feel my aching bones.
—a 14-year-old girl who worked
in a knitting factory, 1936

Where did children work? Many worked in cotton mills. Cotton mills were factories where huge machines used miles and miles of thread to weave cloth. The machines never stopped— night and day, the threads raced from the bobbins.

Little girls called "spinners" had to watch out for breaking threads and quickly tie them together.

Mill owners knew that children with small hands were better at some jobs than adults.

Cherryville, North Carolina. Doffers had to be quick and careful when they replaced bobbins, large spools of thread.

Whenever a bobbin ran out of thread, a boy called a "doffer" would rush to remove the empty bobbin and replace it with a full one. Some of the children in the mills were so small, they had to climb up onto the machines to reach the bobbins.

North Carolina. A young girl works as the foreman stands nearby.

The workers could not take their eyes off the spinning threads for even a minute. One little girl who worked in the mill all night said, "My eyes hurt always from watching the threads at night. Sometimes . . . the threads seem to be cutting into my eyes."

Indianapolis, Indiana. This boy smashed his fingers in a machine in 1908.

Children who worked such long hours did not get enough sleep. Often they ate poorly. They easily became ill. Because they were tired and hungry and bored, they often had accidents. Gears and belts could catch on hair or clothing and pull a child right into the machine.

One doctor in a mill town said that he himself knew over one hundred children who had lost fingers in mill accidents.

Baltimore, Maryland. A boy carries a heavy load of cans.

Factory owners often hired child workers to can fruits and vegetables. Even small children could peel apples or snip beans. Whole families worked together, sometimes from four o'clock in the morning until midnight.

Oyster canneries hired children to open the oyster shells. Boys and girls used sharp knives to pry open the cold, slippery shells. The sharp shells cut fingers, and the juice from the oysters could burn.

Dunbar, Louisiana. A boy named Johnnie stands all day, shucking oysters.

In some factories, children peeled shrimp. The shrimp were kept on ice so they would not spoil. In winter, children had to work in freezing shacks, handling the icy shrimp.

Families who worked in canneries had to travel with the seasons. If they worked in the winter, children could not go to school. Child workers often did not learn to read or write, and they grew up without the skills to find better work.

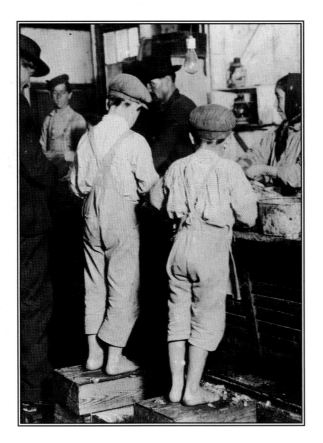

Biloxi, Mississippi. Max, the boy on the right packing shrimp, is eight years old.

Dunbar, Louisiana. At four years of age, Mary shucks two pots of oysters per day.

The man who took this picture asked a little girl who was shucking oysters what her name was. "Dunno," she replied. "How old are you?" he asked. "Dunno," she said again. "How many pots do you shuck in a day?" "Dunno." Is it possible that she truly did not know the answers to his questions?

These mine workers guide mules and carts through tunnels.

Other children went to work far beneath the ground. Coal mines were dark and damp and filled with black dust. There was no light, and the air was very bad. Yet many young boys worked long hours in the dark of the mines.

"Trapper boys" were hired to sit in mine tunnels and open doors for coal cars. The boys had to be careful and very quick: a heavy coal car could not stop if a boy was in the way.

Gary, West Virginia. A trapper stands beside a mine door in 1908.

"Breaker boys" sat on boards above chutes filled with coal. The coal rushed by with a roar on its way to a huge machine that would break it up. The boys reached down to pick out rocks and slate.

Boys sit hunched over piles of coal and rock in the breaker, an unheated building near the mine entrance.

A group of young miners and breaker boys pose for a photograph above ground.

If a boy tumbled in, he could get caught in the machine. At one coal mine, the children were given a half day off work whenever a boy fell and died. But they had to use the half day to attend the dead boy's funeral.

There were many dangers in the mines. Tunnels could cave in or flood. Gases could poison the air and even explode. Breathing coal dust all day hurt the lungs. Accidents were common.

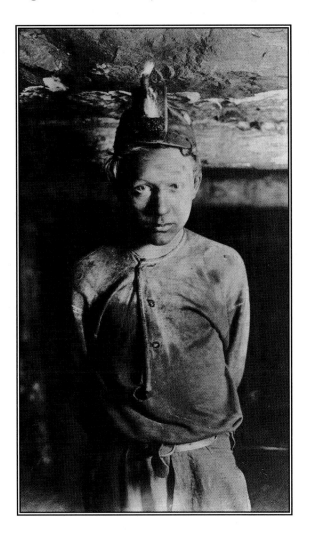

McDonald, West Virginia. More than a mile down into a mine, the light on this trapper boy's cap shines.

Comanche County, Oklahoma. Harold and Jewel Walker are only five and six years old, but they pick between 20 and 25 pounds of cotton each day.

Children who worked outdoors in the fields had sunshine and fresh air to breathe. But it was not easy to work 10 hours a day bending over in the hot sun. On wet days, children with no shoes worked all day in the cold mud.

New York City. In the early morning, two newsboys, ages 11 and 9, start their working day.

In cities, many children worked on the streets. They carried messages, or sold newspapers, or shined shoes. These children were often up late at night and early in the morning. Some stayed away from home for days at a time. Sometimes they became friends with robbers and thieves, who taught them how to steal.

New York City. A family of five works around the kitchen table.

Other city children did their work indoors. Many clothing factories hired people to finish making clothes. Girls and boys sat with their mothers or fathers at home, sewing hour after hour. Or they worked in dark, stuffy factories called sweatshops, with many people in one room. They sewed on buttons or finished seams. They rarely found time to play outside.

Indiana. Even at midnight, these boys are hard at work in a glass factory.

Wherever children worked, they worked hard. There was no time for daydreaming. Many young boys worked in glass factories. Day and night, the red-hot furnaces roared. Boys only eight years old worked as "carry-in boys." They had to run back and forth from the furnace carrying loads of bottles.

A boy pauses near the furnaces during the night shift.

The heat was terrible, over 120 degrees Fahrenheit. Deadly bits of glass powder filled the air. But the boys could not stop to rest. Once, someone measured how far the boys ran every night. The trip to the furnace was one hundred feet long, and each boy made 72 trips back and forth every hour. In eight hours, each boy ran 22 miles.

North Pownal, Vermont. This mill worker, Addie Laird, said she was 12 years old, but the other girls at the mill said she was only 10.

The Fight to End Child Labor

*In the sweatshops . . . the kindergartens are robbed
to provide baby slaves.*
—John Spargo, 1906

Sometimes, when people learned of children who had to work so hard, they tried to stop it. But in the early 1900s, many people thought that hard work was good for children. Sometimes kids had fun working alongside adults. People saw that healthy children had plenty of energy and could do much to help their parents. They thought that children learned new skills when they worked.

In these ways, work can be good. But it is not good when it stops children from growing into strong, happy adults. Children need to play. They need to get enough sleep. They need to eat well. And they need good fresh air and sunshine. In order for their minds to grow, they need to go to school.

For a moment, a young worker turns her back to the machines in a mill.

This cartoon appeared in a magazine in 1913, when Woodrow Wilson was president of the United States. The caption said, "Mr. President, we don't want anything. We just want to grow up."

Reformers were people who wanted to help child workers. They believed that if people knew more about the terrible lives of young workers, they would vote for laws to stop child labor.

These reformers wrote stories for newspapers. They made speeches at churches and clubs and in front of lawmakers. They asked people not to buy things made by children. If everyone stopped buying these things, they said, children would not be needed to make them anymore.

New York City. Women show their opinions on child labor.

Reformers believed that children worked because they were poor. They saw that children who worked did not learn enough to get better jobs when they were older. If all children went to school, reformers said, fewer would grow up to be poor. So reformers worked hard for laws that would make parents send their children to school.

In 1904, the National Child Labor Committee was formed to fight for the end of child labor. Many of the photographs in this book were taken by Lewis Hine, who worked for the committee. His photographs of poor working children showed people the truth. His pictures convinced more and more people that child labor was wrong.

New York City. While taking the picture of a newsboy, reformer and photographer Lewis Hine also captured his own shadow on the sidewalk.

Cincinnati, Ohio. Boys like Sidney Ashcroft, who worked as a bundle carrier, learned few skills.

The National Child Labor Committee helped pass laws in many states to stop children under the age of 14 from working. They passed other laws to stop children under 16 from working more than eight hours a day. Sadly, these laws were not always obeyed.

Philadelphia, Pennsylvania. During a strike of textile workers, these boys took up signs protesting child labor.

In 1916 and in 1919, the United States Congress passed laws to make states end child labor. But the Supreme Court said that Congress could not tell the states what to do. Both laws were struck down.

Finally, in 1938, Congress passed a law called the Fair Labor Standards Act. This time, the Supreme Court did not strike down the law. Under this law, young children were not allowed to work, and older children could not work during school hours. In the years after this law was passed, fewer and fewer children worked.

Left: A weaver sits before her loom in Kathmandu, Nepal.

Right: A boy sells newspapers in Chicago, Illinois. Opposite page: Young brickworkers carry heavy loads in Kathmandu, Nepal.

STILL WORKING FOR PENNIES A DAY

We had to get up at 4 and work 12 hours. We were chained to the looms, but after work we were usually released and could go home to sleep.
—Iqbal Masih, a 12-year-old rug maker in Pakistan, who died in 1995

Around the world, millions of children still work like slaves. In the United States and in many other countries, they work in the fields harvesting crops. They work in sweatshops sewing clothing. In Asian villages, small children sew soccer balls for American children to play with. In Pakistan, they make fancy rugs, tying thousands of tiny knots. They are paid almost nothing. Some are beaten if they try to quit.

What is the answer? Can we put an end to child labor? Laws alone cannot stop it. Many reformers believe that free education for all children should be the first step to ending child labor. But it will not be easy to stop child labor as long as families are very poor and need wages from their children.

Be a Child Labor Detective

Although this book describes American working children of the past, children still work around the world, often in poor and unsafe conditions, and often for very little money. Laws covering child labor are not as strict in some countries as they are in the United States. Some children who work in foreign countries earn money by making things for sale. Like reformers of the past, you can learn about child workers and do something to help them.

Be a child labor detective and investigate whether products made overseas were produced by children.

1. First, educate yourself about child labor in other countries. Where can you find information? Read about child labor in books listed on pages 45 and 46—starting with *Cheap Raw Material: How Our Youngest Workers Are Exploited and Abused* and *Stolen Dreams: Portraits of Working Children*. Go to the library to find up-to-date articles about working children in newspapers and magazines. Explore the Internet, looking at the Websites listed on page 46. Or write to the following organizations for specific information on countries where children work:

United States Committee
 for UNICEF
333 East 38th Street
New York, NY 10016

Bureau of International Labor Affairs
Child Labor Group, Room S-1308
U.S. Department of Labor
Washington, DC 20210

2. How can you find out whether specific products were made by children? Look at the packaging or labels to find out the address of the maker. Write a letter to ask how the product is made. Your letter might look something like this:

[your address]

[date]

Dear Sir or Madam:

I am concerned about the use of child labor in making products sold in the United States. I would like to know where your product is made and whether children helped to make it.

Can you tell me if children helped to make your product? Is there any organization that will certify, or prove, that products like yours were made by adults?

Thank you for any information you can give me.

Sincerely yours,

[your name]

3. When you receive a reply, follow up on the information you get. If there is an organization that will certify, or prove, that child labor wasn't used to make the product, write to that organization. Ask about the products and the companies that interest you.

4. Once you have gathered information about a company or product, think about ways you can use your new knowledge to make a difference. For instance, should you write thank-you letters to companies that don't use child labor? Should you tell other people what you have learned? Should you boycott products that are made by children? What are the disadvantages of boycotts? (Sometimes child workers lose jobs and earnings when people stop buying products children produce.) Should you ask politicians here and in foreign countries to end child labor and to support free schooling for all?

NOTE TO TEACHERS AND ADULTS

For modern children, the lives of working children in the early 1900s may seem like part of a far-off past. But there are many ways to make this era and its people come alive. One way is to read more about children who worked. More books on the topic are listed on pages 45 and 46. Another way to explore the past is to train young readers to study historical photographs. Historical photographs hold many clues about how life was lived in earlier times.

Ask your children or students to look for the details and "read" all the information in each picture in this book. For example, why do so many of the girls shown working in textile mills wear their hair short or in braids? (Along with being fashionable, this style kept hair away from the machinery, so girls were not accidentally pulled into the gears.) To learn to read historical photographs, have young readers try these activities:

All Kinds of Work

Study the photographs of working children in this book. On a piece of paper in one column, under the heading "Early 1900s," write down all the different kinds of jobs you see children doing. Next, set aside time after school or on a weekend and interview your parents. Find out what kinds of jobs, from household chores to paid work, they did when they were children. Under the heading "My Parents' Time," write down these jobs. In a third column, under the heading "Today," write down all the kinds of work you do. What conclusions can you draw about how children's work has changed? Would your parents be happy to have you do the work they did as children?

Writing Letters

Lewis Hine met many children while investigating and taking photographs of child labor. The photographs on the cover of this book and on pages 1, 2, 5, 7–13, 15–21, 24–30, 32, 35, and 36 were all taken by Hine. From the point of view, or perspective, of one of the child workers pictured on those pages, write a letter to Lewis Hine and the National Child Labor Committee. Describe the place where you work, the kind of work you do, and the hours you work. Are you treated fairly? What kind of changes would you like to see at your workplace? Describe yourself as well. How old are you? How long have you worked?

To learn more about Hine and how his photographs changed views about child labor, read *Kids at Work: Lewis Hine and the Crusade against Child Labor.*

Growing Up As a Working Kid

Choose one of the working children pictured in this book. Then dress in costume and tell your friends, parents, or classmates what your life is like. Try to answer these questions: What kind of work do you do? When must you get up in the morning? How long do you work? Do you know how to read and write? Is your job dangerous? Do you want to work? Do you have a choice?

For information and details about the lives of working children, read the text—and the photos—in this book. To add to your presentation, read some of the books on child labor on pages 45 and 46. If you are playing the part of a factory worker, read *Fire at the Triangle Factory*, a story about Minnie, a girl who works in a clothing factory. If you are playing the part of a breaker boy in a coal mine, take a look at *Growing Up in Coal Country*, a book about children who worked in Pennsylvania's coal mines and breakers.

Resources on Working Children

Bartoletti, Susan Campbell. *Growing Up in Coal Country*. Boston: Houghton Mifflin Company, 1996. Using interviews, newspapers, and other sources, Bartoletti examines the lives of children who worked in Pennsylvania coal mines in the late 1800s and early 1900s.

Currie, Stephen. *We Have Marched Together: The Working Children's Crusade*. Minneapolis, Minn.: Lerner Publications Company, 1997. Currie follows a group of working children who marched from Philadelphia to New York in 1903 with labor leader Mary "Mother" Jones to publicize the abuses of child labor.

Freedman, Russell. *Kids at Work: Lewis Hine and the Crusade against Child Labor*. New York: Clarion Books, 1994. Freedman tells the story of Lewis Hine, a former teacher who traveled the country taking pictures of working children. Hine's photographs helped to change public opinion—and laws—about children and work.

Hakim, Joy. *An Age of Extremes*. New York: Oxford University Press, 1994. Part of a series on United States history, this book looks at people who lived in the late 1800s and early 1900s and includes chapters on child labor.

Littlefield, Holly. Illustrated by Mary O'Keefe Young. *Fire at the Triangle Factory*. Minneapolis, Minn.: Carolrhoda Books, Inc., 1996. Fourteen-year-old Minnie has worked in a factory since she was ten. Now she and her best friend, Tessa, run sewing machines that make fancy blouses. At the end of a long working day, fire breaks out in the crowded factory, and the two friends must find their way to safety.

Meltzer, Milton. *Cheap Raw Material: How Our Youngest Workers Are Exploited and Abused.* New York: Viking, 1994. Meltzer explores the deep roots of child labor, beginning with the enslavement of children in ancient times and continuing in the present around the world.

Parker, David L., with Lee Engfer and Robert Conrow. *Stolen Dreams: Portraits of Working Children.* Minneapolis, Minn.: Lerner Publications Company, 1998. Author and photographer Parker shows the stark world of modern working children in India, Nepal, Bangladesh, Indonesia, Mexico, and the United States.

Paterson, Katherine. *Lyddie.* New York: Lodestar Books, 1991. In this novel, a young girl named Lyddie leaves farm life behind to become a mill worker.

Saller, Carol. Illustrated by Ken Green. *Florence Kelley.* Minneapolis, Minn.: Carolrhoda Books, Inc., 1997. The story of Florence Kelley, a tireless opponent of child labor, is interspersed with brief descriptions of actual working children.

Websites about Working Children

http://usa.ilo.org/ilowbo/ilokids/index.html
Part of the official Website of the International Labor Organization, ILO Kids explains what child labor is and isn't, offers examples of goods produced by children, and provides information on what children can do to help end child labor.

http://www.digtalrag.com/iqbal/index.html
After students at Broadmeadow Middle School in Massachusetts met Iqbal Masih, a Pakistani rug worker who fought to end child labor, they started the Kids Campaign to Build a School for Iqbal. This Website follows their progress in building a school in Pakistan and in fighting to end child labor around the world.

New Words

child labor: when children of school age work long hours or do work that is not safe or legal

Fair Labor Standards Act: a 1938 federal law that set the following rules: Children younger than 14 can work only in some farming jobs, in newspaper delivery, and in acting. Children must be 16 to work in a factory or to work during school hours. No one younger than 18 can be hired for certain dangerous or harmful jobs.

reformers: people who take action to change things that they think are bad or wrong

sweatshop: a workplace that is hidden in a house or building so that the owners do not have to follow the laws that protect workers

Index

TIME LINE

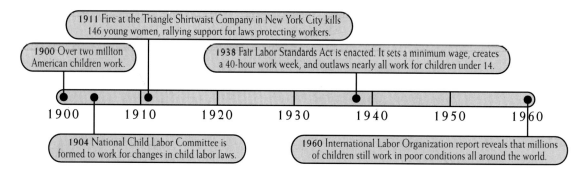

1911 Fire at the Triangle Shirtwaist Company in New York City kills 146 young women, rallying support for laws protecting workers.

1900 Over two million American children work.

1938 Fair Labor Standards Act is enacted. It sets a minimum wage, creates a 40-hour work week, and outlaws nearly all work for children under 14.

1900 1910 1920 1930 1940 1950 1960

1904 National Child Labor Committee is formed to work for changes in child labor laws.

1960 International Labor Organization report reveals that millions of children still work in poor conditions all around the world.

ABOUT THE AUTHOR

Carol Fisher Saller is an editor and writer who lives in Chicago with her husband, Richard, and two sons, John and Ben. There, she enjoys gardening, singing in a choir, and listening to her boys play their electric guitars.

Ms. Saller's interest in child labor arose from her work on a biography of Florence Kelley, a reformer who fought for laws to protect children. Saller saw Lewis Hine's eloquent black-and-white photographs of working children and wanted to learn more about the lives of young workers in the past. Recent news stories about child labor—in the United States and around the world—inspired her to write this book.

PHOTO ACKNOWLEDGMENTS

The photographs in this book appear through the courtesy of: Library of Congress, front and back cover, pp. 1, 2, 5, 9, 10, 11, 12, 13, 15, 16, 17, 18, 19, 20, 21, 22, 24, 26, 28, 29, 32, 35, 36; Brown Brothers, Sterling, PA, 18463, pp. 6, 23, 31, 34; Corbis-Bettmann, pp. 7, 8, 25, 27, 37; North Carolina Division of Archives and History, p. 14; National Archives, neg. # 102-LH-1056, p. 30; IPS, p. 33; David L. Parker, pp. 38 (both), 39; Linda Erf Swift, p. 48.